THE WHISPERING SKY

PREVIOUS COLLECTIONS BY RICHARD KELL

Fantasy Poets 35 (pamphlet, Oxford 1957)
Control Tower (1962)
Differences (1969)
Humours (1978)
Heartwood (pamphlet,1978)
The Broken Circle (1981)
In Praise of Warmth, New & Selected (1987)
Rock and Water (1993)
Collected Poems (2001)
Under the Rainbow (2003)
Letters to Enid (2004)
Taking a Break (2008)
Hilarity and Wonder (2011)
Old Man Answering (2014)
Making Word Gifts (2016)

THE WHISPERING SKY

RICHARD KELL

All rights reserved. No part of this work covered by the copyright herein may be reproduced or used in any means—graphic, electronic, or mechanical, including copying, recording, taping, or information storage and retrieval systems—without written permission of the publisher.

Printed by imprintdigital
Upton Pyne, Exeter
www.digital.imprint.co.uk

Typesetting by narrator
www.narrator.me.uk
info@narrator.me.uk
033 022 300 39

Published by Shoestring Press
19 Devonshire Avenue, Beeston, Nottingham, NG9 1BS
(0115) 925 1827
www.shoestringpress.co.uk

First published 2020
© Copyright: Richard Kell
© Cover design by Becky Saunders
© Author photograph by Sammy Jetter Kell

The moral right of the author has been asserted.

ISBN 978-1-912524-50-1

In loving memory of my elder brother Donald
and my younger brother Alan

CONTENTS

I

On the Ocean Wave	3
Deities	4
A Promise Kept	5
The Beauty of Life	6
Lives	7
A News Report	8
All the Way down	9
No Chewing Needed	10
Providence	11
The Origin of Humankind	12
Themes for the Bard	13
Fucking	14
The Culprit	15
A Triad	16
Disintegration	19
Water	23

II

The Genetic Lottery	27
Relief	28
Please Explain	29
Two Ways?	30
Still Trying to Understand Relativity	31
On Being Stuck with My Familiar Self	32
Prospects	34
What Are We?	35

III

Literacy Now	39
The Growth of Language	40
The Ghost in the Machine	41
A Troublesome Word	42
An Imagined Reply from a Novelist	43

The Language of Poetry	44
To Some Poets	45
Rough Reading	46
Reader Taking Trouble	47
Production Lines	49
Odd Work	50
G for George	51
Between Poems	52
Against Flights of Poesy	53
Facing the Epics	54
Fame: A Duologue	57

IV

Colour Coding	61
A Bit Deaf	63
To a Walking-Stick	64
A Plea for Assisted Dying	65
Charities	67
Thinking of Death	68
Liberation	69
Letting Go	70
A Friendly Fiasco	71
An Anxious Reply	72

*

A note on the title of this book	74

I

ON THE OCEAN WAVE

for John Lucas at eighty

Clipper and man-o'-war: enchanting, yes!
At twelve I was beguiled
by 'Whither, O splendid ship …' It took a while,
with the help of *Dauber* and other tales,
to find the loveliness
no more than scenic, a gift of hull and sails
and bow-sliced foaming water. Life on board
was rough at best, hellish when hurricane
or storm of battle roared.
Is 'Sea Fever' sentimental, an old hand's
nostalgia filtering out the pain?
Anyway, as youngsters we had green islands
and cobbled seaports, were matey with yo-ho crews,
drank rum in taverns, and even sinned
deliciously in stews.
Later, philosophy ghosted us a Ship
of Destiny or of Hope, and fickle wind
had meaning. Steam gave symbolism the slip.
What images have we now,
the grand sails gone for ever? Can
the nose of a plane or a rocket match a prow
and its figurehead in fabling the quests of Man?

Note: This poem was included in the birthday anthology *Strike Up the Band* (2017), ed. Merryn Williams.

DEITIES

for Peter Radcliffe

Dionysus seems the friendliest god. While Zeus
hurls thunderbolts and Ares kindles war,
his genial visits grant us an excuse
to drink and revel, let our spirits soar
to rapturous heights. But then
we feel ourselves being dragged toward Pluto's den.
We envy the Olympians their laughter,
so far above the miseries of men
whose joyous nights are mocked by mornings-after,
and of a king who thought the wine-god grim,
torn by his mother's Maenads limb from limb.

A PROMISE KEPT

At the gate of the city, Tamburlaine
declared 'If you open up,
I promise not to stain
your precincts with a single drop
of blood.' Seeing they couldn't win—
could never hope to drive
such massive power away, or rid
themselves by other means—they let him in.
Then, what the great man scrupulously did
was bury his hosts alive.

THE BEAUTY OF LIFE

In documentaries about all sorts of things—
cosmology, astronomy, wildlife, medicine, food
et cetera—I hear presenters again and again
saying 'beautiful'. A blunder. Since its meaning
is 'full of beauty', it's logically objective,
but as used by these enthusiasts it's clearly
the opposite, giving no more than a writer-presenter
feels about something or other because his researches
have moved him to that feeling, which is commonly
and logically expressed by 'amazing', 'wonderful',
'mind-boggling', 'awesome' and so on. It both amused
and enraged me when a scientist rhapsodized
about the beautiful miracle of life
and the chances, backed by the beautiful Drake equation,
of conscious beings on millions of other planets.
Is he mad? Has his quasi-monastic seclusion for years
in a physics lab prevented him from seeing
that life known here, though a generative process,
has been no less a callously violent one
causing alarm and horror across the globe
for creatures great and small equipped with nerves?
Accidental or planned (another problem),
it isn't a thing of beauty to be enjoyed,
but a tragedy to deplore. I wish the dust
from bursting stars had vanished into the Void.

LIVES

Pakistan's Streets of Shame: TV report
whose facts were piercing as a heartfelt cry.
I asked a void what sort
of fathers could rely
on little sons to earn sufficient pay
picking through garbage fourteen hours a day.

Stuff for recycling. If they don't collect
enough rupees'-worth, parents will be cross
and then they can expect
a beating. Gain and loss
are paramount for families who endure
day after day the curse of being poor.

Some youngsters run away, live on the street.
By night the drivers at a terminus
will offer them 'a treat'
(drugs) for brute intercourse.
'They do bad things' one haunted victim said—
without a home, a mother's care, a bed.

Folk who do care discovered he'd a knife
with which, despairing, he had stabbed his arm.
They hope to change his life,
divert him from self-harm.
'Life is a precious gift' they tell a boy
who's learned it is a force that can destroy.

A NEWS REPORT

That TV moment comes to me again:
small boy in the Middle East,
his hands an image out of sci-fi
horror, grotesquely large.
At school he's mocked, a monster.

'It is the will of God' his father says.
His uncle declares that evil spirits
have entered him. 'They breed in the latrine.'
The small boy waits, desperate and bewildered,
while doctors and surgeons wonder what to do.

ALL THE WAY DOWN

another for Thorn Gruin

"Big fleas have little fleas
upon their backs to bite 'em"—
nonsense that made a point. Here's
a less fantastic item
(gleaned from a science mag)
to astonish and inspire us.
The *sputnik virophag*
is a 'fellow-travelling' virus
that feeds on a bigger one,
the *mamavirus*. What
bizarre Darwinian fun!
Disease, it seems, can rot,
as well as apes and kings,
weird parasitic things
far tinier than a dot.

NO CHEWING NEEDED

A thin slimy tube
the screen first showed alone
is now a red leech
pursuing a blue worm
as long as itself.

Next moment its mouth is fixed
around the worm's rear end
and has started sucking.
The forward end
lashes in panicked rage.

That meal slides through, alive—
has become, when the mouth closes,
a perfect inner tube.
The outer won't fill again
for at least a month.

PROVIDENCE

The water goes, the grass, the leafy shade.
Starved and thirsty, elephants feebly plod.
A female drops. Her little son, dismayed,
not knowing that she is dying,
urges her with his trunk. Then come the lions.
All, with ignorant innocence, are relying
on Nature, who works for God.

THE ORIGIN OF HUMANKIND

Organic evolution, we've been taught,
depended in the first place
on random changes. A few would bring about
traits in the forebears of, say, moss and mice
by which they'd adapt to changed environment
and so be 'selected' for survival.
Chance and fitness then, no deep intent
of a universal spirit, good or evil.

Consider, when its aeon came,
the desire to fuck and be fucked
so creatures could engender more of the same.
If anticipation and achievement lacked
pleasure there could be no desire, so how
did the pleasure start? By chance?
Then, equally by chance, there might have been no
such thrill, therefore no coupling to advance
a species, hence no further evolution.
It seems to me that Darwinists who add
the anthropic principle risk the strange conclusion
that sexual joy 'just happened' because it had to.

*

PS: The last line's teaser may be wrong.
Does 'anthropic' say that humans *would* exist
or *could*? Anyway, please enjoy the twist,
a clinch-knot for a thoughtful kind of song.

THEMES FOR THE BARD

An Ode to Sexual Joy? Fine.
To Sexual Fun? Perhaps.
But they'd suggest the difference between
deep diving and shallow dips.

Those who judged all carnal delight
ungodly were trapped by faith,
but even the paganly passionate
knew that taking the path
to lust's relief—no more a sin
than eating—offered less,
being selfish, than to share the one
leading to lovers' bliss.

A thoughtful cynic scowls:
"For sexual joy or fun
we once were Nature's fools.
How else could she begin
each round of propagation
and worrying parenthood?
Though dodgy, contraception
also deserves an ode."

FUCKING

The act that God decreed
so great and small could breed
is, as I see it, both
sublime and fit for mirth,
no less suggestive of
quaint plumbing than of love.

THE CULPRIT

Please let me speak once more about our vague
folk-wisdom, referring this time to the Plague.
Those putrid sores no rituals or drugs
could get the better of were caused by bugs
from rats that made their homes where dirt was rife.
What Black so well described was really Life.

A TRIAD

(1) **Rhapsody in Black**

I've sometimes felt it would be good to die,
or fall into dreamless sleep and never wake,
relieved at last of the darkest question, *why*:
why humans seem outrageous, a mistake
of God or Cosmos—creatures more than smart
at physics and genetics, nuts and bolts,
buildings, transport, highways, language, art,
clothing and food and weapons, yet such dolts
in worship and morality, trying and trying
so hard for centuries, never finding the way
to peaceful joy. Instead, prone to decrying,
envying, vaunting, bickering, slipping from play
to fear and fury. Why were we made like this
or evolved like this? *Sapiens?* What a laugh!
The peak of creation? More like a grim abyss.
The ant, the snake, the penguin and the giraffe
are fitter for the planet than we are.
Okay, we have a house with central heating,
washing machine, TV; we drive a car;
the shopping mall provides delicious eating;
our years increase along with better health.
Think of the Middle Ages, the disease,
torchlight and gloom in alleys full of filth,
candle-lit chambers shared with rats and fleas.
We've electricity, intricate sanitation,
capable doctors, nurses: we've progressed!
But are we happier now than any nation
or empire of past ages, East or West?
I doubt it. Try comparing modern lives
with what we know of all that went before.
Indoors are fractious siblings, husbands, wives,
outdoors political rancour, protest, war,
and in our hearts continuing discontent,
'the quarrel with ourselves' because we're human.

We're often kind, our dealings are well meant,
we recognize that we've a lot in common,
so black can be relieved with streaks of grey.
But pain's the norm, and though scared millions pray,
their God, incomparable Father-King,
stays absolutely silent and does nothing.

(2) Any Takers?

Life is as bad as God. On every side
you see it prized, praised, worshipped. Now the tide
of human longing spreads through stellar space.
Its eagerness to find some distant place
where life is doing its stuff, as here on earth,
imbues me with a mix of rage and mirth.
Is it because we're living that we crawl
before a vital power whose ways appal,
and rail instead at death although it's plain
that death does nothing? What we call the pain
of dying involves one life against another
when creatures dangerously come together
(from human to microbial), or some vast
convulsion of the earth (volcanic blast
or earthquake—not alive but no less grim)
mocks every dogma, every prayer and hymn
that honours God and Life. How odd we are,
cramped on one planet of a minor star,
so clever yet such biocentric fools,
looking for destiny in nature's rules.
Are there some other worlds, remote from ours,
where lives are shaped by less malignant powers?
Deep probes may find there are, but why the fuss?
Here, waiting for a sign, we've only us
to catch a hint of purpose if we can.
The anthropic principle? Was it for Man
that cosmic tuning and the long ascent
from quark to cell and then to brain were meant?
Unlikely, but who knows? What we *do* know
is that the evolutionary flow,

with law-bound subtle turbulence, has made
a species both resourceful and afraid,
desperate but striving on, its politics
and ethics an unmanageable mix
of idealism and pragmatism, a will
to co-exist and a willingness to kill.
We bear calamities with 'C'est la vie',
'Shit happens' or, when pious hearts agree,
'Behold the wrath of God'. And still we cling
to life though *it*'s the monster with the sting,
while death ensures that when our breath has gone
we'll rest in peace, in pure oblivion.

(3) **A Reply**

Who knows, indeed! So why the rage and mirth?
Here's a less fiery thought for what it's worth.
If human life looks no more special than
a mushroom's or a microbe's when you scan
the biosphere and then the vast array
of inorganic stuff, from gas to clay,
that came before it, aren't you almost blind?
Surely you can't ignore the work of mind:
great music, painting, poetry, science (though
that gnaws at faith!), and what our nations owe
to surgery, architecture, engineering.
No, I don't like your nihilistic sneering.
I'd grant the more we know the more we doubt
when wondering what life is all about:
conviction's not my way. But I have hope.
I'll never join you on the slippery slope
that ends in black negation and despair.
I'll walk on level ground, still try to care
for things long cherished by the simple heart,
including trust, compassion, friendship, art.

DISINTEGRATION

Too much, dear God!—
creatures and things, works
of nature and of mind,
all ending beneath the sod
for probing teams to find.
Those friends and the rest of us,
with our many gifts and quirks,
our habits and habitats,
will be destroyed. That's
on one small planet lit
by one small star. Add
the countless annihilations,
the ending of every bit
throughout a cosmos: sad,
tragic, preposterous!
What meaning can be found
in such profusion, all
those intricate conformations
that entropy will untie?
Questions like that appal;
answers go round and round,
keep coming back to *Why*.

    I've nothing to submit
but this: that there's a single
energy we call
the universe, every 'thing'
is a part of it, so they all
subtly intermingle.
Energy can't be destroyed,
but 'things', by the second law
of thermodynamics, will fray
to a vast chaotic void
offering not even raw
material from which
(unless by 'divine play',
an idea some Hindus share)

new order could be created.
No consolation there,
given that every stitch
of evolution is fated
to be undone.
               Go back
to what we started with,
the fact of profusion and death,
and the disconcerting lack
of meaning, so it seems,
in such discordance. Add
the thought that though we mean
so much to ourselves and then
to each other, and human schemes
look special, as though they had
that sacredness tribe and state
have cherished for so long,
a value to celebrate
in 'holy' war and song:
how does all that appear
whenever we contemplate
the magnitude of space,
and then the smallness of
the proton, in relation
to our beloved sphere?
Where's the 'below', the 'above'
that fixed a unique place
for *sapiens* with his humble
pride, fear, consecration?
Age-old certainties crumble,
and we like them will be all
near-sediment in the sprawl
of a cosmos fading away
to a tenuous quantal mist
where nothing more can decay.
Then, only stilled
energy will exist,
no power that could start to build
a world that might include

creatures as well as things,
let alone minds imbued
with awe of heavenly kings
and angels.
    But listen to this,
though maybe you won't agree:
In the last analysis
we confront a mystery free
from our need to solve, to *know*.
Let be, let be,
let the stream of unthinking flow!
Or welcome nihilists
and absurdists, with their plea
that only the Void persists—
from which, inanely, sprang
crude energy with a bang
followed by vast inflation,
then violence continuing in
extravagant evolution,
till creatures formed whose lives,
ruled by impulsive drives,
were edged with pain.
Some in the end were blessed
with a fertile sapient brain
that invented God and sin,
philosophy, politics, art,
machinery, and at last
work that put to the test
with experimental precision
theories dismissed as smart
and empty by orthodox goofs
in turn exposed to derision
by unassailable proofs.
  Physics: hooray, alas!
Einstein's famous equation
would make it clear that mass
is energy in disguise.
Compare what Kant believed,
and mystical searchers too:

that appearance lies.
The truths of commonsense,
rooted in what's perceived,
for here and now will do,
but beyond? Oh the immense
unknown that the scientist
works hard to learn at least
a part of, leaving behind
(sorry again!) the priest
with his godly book and list
of rights and wrongs designed
for folk hoping to fly
to Paradise when they die.
Here for a while we are,
truth-seekers made of dust
from some exploded star,
in a world that will rot away,
entropically undone.
    I like rather than trust—
his mind being apt to stray
from seriousness to fun—
what an old poet says:
that everything there is,
each transient 'it' and 'me'
so real-seeming,
exists as a kind of dreaming
in the depth of a nameless One
that will always be.

WATER

This, like other good things,
just came along. But being such vital stuff,
so pure, so deliciously throat-soothing,
no wonder it seemed given,
when they hadn't withdrawn in a huff,
by spirits, then thunderous divine kings
on mountain-tops or in heaven.

I think of that as I lift my glass,
but then of the first
explosion, energy becoming mass
in the Higgs Field, and after billions of years
a cold clear liquid slaking the thirst
of animals. Then of the ones,
capable of speech and tears,
who frequently thought in metaphors
but literally of bows, later of guns
and other treasures for waging wars.
God helped one side or the other,
so water and wine,
though amply available to both,
they took in tribal pride as a sign
of aid from above. Such a sapient muddle!

But are we luckier seeing as a riddle
that may have no solution
the fact of cosmic growth,
eventually life and mind and their evolution?
Anyway, after an unimaginable lapse
of time some genius began to think
of fluids being conveyed through pipes and taps.
Now even the godless can fill a glass and drink.

II

THE GENETIC LOTTERY

'Bone idle' we sometimes hear,
perhaps 'born idle'. Both,
though tersely eloquent, miss the truth:
'bone lazy' is more accurate.

Laziness and fear
frequently mix. They're in the bone,
the blood, the spirit, God knows what,
even before a person's born.

Genes are to blame for that,
not Adam or us. I propose a medal
(gold) to be proudly worn
by every lazybones who is far from idle.

No!—I'm forgetting will.
That too is randomly given, strong or weak.
But at least they can feel proud, each Jack and Jill,
if they think it matters more, to be unique.

RELIEF

No need, thank God, to brave the rain.
But how unmanly! Real men
have always eagerly left the den
and gladly endured whatever pain
harshness of weather or terrain
has caused them.—Gladly? H'm… I guess
they've often longed for the end of stress
that sleep would bring. Oates, we're told,
a moment before he left the tent
to plunge out into horrific cold,
said 'I may be some time', and sadly
we all know what he meant.

PLEASE EXPLAIN

I like, since it seems to let me off the hook,
Buddhism's *anatta* (no-self) doctrine. This
suggests that in the last analysis
my sins were committed by a kind of spook
or will-o'-the wisp, not by a real me.
What a relief to learn that all the deeds
I now deplore—a child of western creeds—
weren't really mine; to know that I am free
from guilt as husband, father, brother, friend,
professional man and neighbour. But although
the doctrine's comforting I can't outgrow
the feeling that it's I who in the end
must bear the blame for failures.—That aside,
I wish some Buddhist priest would help me see
how *anatta* and *samsara* can agree.
If there's no self, what is it, when I've died,
that will return unmindful of its past
(how many lives?—how long the karmic chain?)
to find a way once more through harsh terrain,
hoping to feel the ocean's breath at last.

TWO WAYS?

Again I read that things are not as they seem,
that all are made of energy ever shifting.

Again I see the lovely self-composure
of objects in my room, and they bring to mind
those eloquent still life paintings by the masters.

Oh masters of the spirit and of the senses,
do you really disagree so radically?

Must I choose between the stillness of a bowl,
called *maya*, and the hidden dance that's known
as *lila*, suchness, probability waves?

No: if energy's real, so is glass—
quick change in slow ('stillness') one cosmic flow.

STILL TRYING TO UNDERSTAND RELATIVITY

My coffee being stirred went round and round.
According to Mach and Einstein—Berkeley too—
its tiny circling meant that it was bound
to every other object we can view,
the galaxies included. As I drink,
that milky prelude makes me think and think.

ON BEING STUCK WITH MY FAMILIAR SELF

(1)

How captivating the Dalai Lama is,
so affable and humorous, also brighter
than modesty can claim, in fact a whiz
as a modern-minded writer
on Buddhist thought and practice. I've been reading
How To See Yourself As You Really Are,
a book which, early on, advises heeding
the truth that real things (we're offered 'car')
aren't *really* real: each is merely Form
and therefore Emptiness. So far so good;
but when exact instructions start to swarm
for how to see without being fooled, the wood
gets hidden by the trees.
In meditation there's so much to do—
physical, mental—that it's quite a tease,
like trying to join wet surfaces with glue.
And oh, you have to persevere for days
and weeks and months and years for liberation
from the tormenting maze
of 'cyclic existence' (once 'reincarnation').
That's fine if you're a specialist, a monk
like the endearing author of these pages,
but their requirements leave me in a funk.
Only my wishful discontent engages—
which means, alas, I'll very likely sin
for lifetimes till I learn self-discipline.

(2)

Dear Tenzin (if I may):
Reading your friendly book from end to end
I've granted 'yes'—not once but fifty times!—
to everything you say
describing how a serious person climbs
rung after rung of wisdom to transcend
the ignorance that causes our dismay.
The trouble is you never say what 'I'
goes on from life to life. Until you do
I won't believe reincarnation's true.
The self that seems to die
is nothing more than 'form' you tell me. Yes!
But then what self that *isn't* emptiness
will be the one that fastens old to new?

PROSPECTS

Within the nonsense of reincarnation
(How, reduced to a reptile's, could my behaviour
be 'good' in ways to lift me back towards human?)
there's a bright grain of sense: each life gives hope
we might be freed at last from a chain of lives
into some kind of heaven.—Utterly different,
the most horrific idea yet conceived,
is eternal recurrence, everything happening again
and again and again, down to the smallest detail.
My life would be part of that, its tests and failures
meaninglessly replayed for ever and ever.
Yes, there'd be happy moments, but what else
could make this a kinder hell than the priestly one?
Oh comfort me, some angel: tell me it's false
to say there's nothing new under the sun.

WHAT ARE WE?

(written after reading a book review)

According to some ancient Hindu thinkers
    brahman is pure consciousness
and the world, including us, is what it's dreaming.

Now I read that a modern metaphysician,
    Chalmers, 'suspects that consciousness
is a primal aspect of our universe',

and *brahman*—though not mentioned—here becomes
    'a godlike cyber-entity'
that we are all 'the software constructs of'.

Nothing about our dying. What happens then?
    Are we deleted in some way,
or stored as thinner software in the Cloud?

Trendy stuff. I'm intrigued and flummoxed by
    the thought of adoring Top Computer.
What might Shankara say if he's still around?

Note: The book referred to—reviewed in *New Scientist* 12 November 2016—is *The Singularity*, edited by Uziel Awret.

III

LITERACY NOW

Help! Help! Help!
My terror overflows.
Grim tentacles of kelp
are groping at my limbs,
and water brims my nose.
My sight's becoming blear,
my understanding dims,
and scraps of plaintive hymns
hum in my mental ear.
May one who boats or swims
come close enough to hear
my desperate gurgling yelp
and kindly rescue me,
haul me clear of a sea
acrid with acronyms.

THE GROWTH OF LANGUAGE

Our abstract words are mostly
rooted in metaphor.
Here's one delightful instance
(you've met a hundred more!):
longing, a gem of speech
that came from the fact of distance
and good things out of reach.
When brains first worked at bits
of telling that were ghostly,
they drew on their five wits.

THE GHOST IN THE MACHINE

With the best of intentions
the stickler in my laptop
put a green squiggle under
the sentence I had typed.
'Why?' I pleaded. 'Neither
vocabulary nor grammar
seems faulty.' Then (NB)
I noticed 'then' and 'while'
in the same construction. Was that
a worry my cyber-mate was too
inflexible to endure?

Here was one of those words
so humble and familiar
we use them unaware of
their versatility. 'It was then
that all seemed lost; but then …'
—four letters offering 'at that time'
and 'afterwards': how strange!
Dear logical ignorant minder,
thank you for showing me yet again
that well-worn bits of speech can be
as quirky as they're plain.

A TROUBLESOME WORD

'Chance' will do for probability:
you can say 'the chances are',
or 'the odds'. But what does it mean to say
'by chance' or 'a chance event'?

Take, for example, car accidents.
They're thought of as events
happening by chance. But all
have been caused in ways known or unknown.

The driver here had a heart attack.
There a little boy ran out.
This car skidded on ice. Those two
collided because of bad overtaking.

How about the *Titanic*?
Accident yes, coincidence yes,
chance no. Two speeds and courses
brought steel and ice inexorably together.

Experiments with quanta that are 'entangled'
find very strange causation. When something's done
to one particle of a pair, the other reacts
immediately though it's a thousand miles away.

The tumbling of dice is mechanical, so the outcome
of every throw can in principle be predicted.
Einstein, harrier of the fortuitists,
used the wrong metaphor in his note on God!

Perhaps each happening adds to a web of causes,
including choices, woven since time began—
whose every stitch would be known, Laplace maintained,
if a cosmic super-intelligence could observe it.

AN IMAGINED REPLY FROM A NOVELIST

I'm sorry my book 'dismayed a devotee',
but no, I can't be sorry that I wrote it.

I felt I had a right—that I was free—
to dig away at freedom-blocking dirt.

Which of us, since your holy man's decree
blasted my life, has been more deeply hurt?

THE LANGUAGE OF POETRY

When was it that the arbiters of taste,
for fear of being disgraced
as nincompoops, began to praise
what, though artistically pure,
was also bafflingly obscure,
fine lines creating a linguistic maze?

Now, it appears, we've reached the stage
where every cryptic poet is a sage,
even a mage. It seems a run
of syllables that makes no sense
offers a deep experience,
as though a web of wisdom has been spun.

Pure music can achieve
something like that. But words, though they can weave
melodies of a kind, all have their own
proud meanings which, unless
they're firmly linked, make a semantic mess
whose vibes will bore some listeners to the bone.

TO SOME POETS

What *are* you trying to say?
I'm working hard, but though a ray
of understanding, so of hope,
glimmers occasionally, still I grope
in desperation. Oh, I feel so dim,
so simple-minded! Nursery rhyme and hymn
are all I'm fit for.—No, that can't be right.
I've read a thousand poems, neither trite
nor slack, that haven't gone against the grain,
that haven't dulled my heart and racked my brain.
Are you among the moderns who believe
a poet need only weave
textures of imagery and sound,
that these can have profound
significance without what people mean
by meaning? Have you been
enthralled by Stevens, Ashbery and Prynne?

I too love verbal music, but deny
that words themselves are spell-like. Why
was language born if not to communicate
for welfare and survival? To narrate
was part of that: the comic and the tragic
could give imagining a kind of magic
when words made sense-linked sentences and these
made tales and fantasies,
in which at times the otherworlds of cloven
hoof and golden wing were interwoven
enchantingly. And how,
unless the I-and-thou
that is the ground of speech
was kept, could that be done, the poem reach
a listener's mind and heart?
Please tell me how *your* art,
which lacks what meaning seems to mean, is meant.
I've really tried. Forgive my discontent.

ROUGH READING

Five hundred pages. I've wrestled maybe a third.
Whatever they're trying to say is hopelessly blurred.

This river I've ventured onto raves and bullies.
My canoe is tumbled by white-water humps and gullies.

Pope wasn't like this, or Wordsworth, Keats, Hardy,
Larkin … None was so wild, so monstrously wordy.

I stay afloat only with desperate expertise:
the blades of my paddle are gasping *please please please*.

Relief at last. Water that's not so rough?
No, I've shut the book. Enough is enough.

READER TAKING TROUBLE

'If it isn't difficult it's no good.' – A pundit.

In novels you will meet
a paragraph at times
which, though it has no feet,
no symmetry, no rhymes,
is more delightful than
a page of lines that scan.

Rereading cryptic verse
by some of the modern greats
I feel impelled to curse.
But diffidence frustrates
my anger: who am I
to snarl? Instead I sigh.

But oh that sigh is deep:
my efforts to understand
are putting me to sleep.
We don't want stuff that's bland,
but why again and again
must I torment my brain?

Which of us is the dolt,
this eminent bard or me?
I remember 'A fool's bolt
is soon shot', and agree
it may be mine. But no,
surely that can't be so!

Once more I scrutinize
a celebrated work,
reputedly so wise
and yet so full of murk—
substantial writing, yes,
but in detail such a mess.

Would a family-archive note
make this allusion plain?
Here bits of grammar float:
I've laboured, but in vain,
to mend what looks like blether
by fitting them together.

Where logic has been smudged
fine phrases are at war.
Now, equally misjudged,
a mazy metaphor
so thrills the heart that mind,
demurring, will seem blind.

Clauses entangled, lexis
misleading, scansion odd:
oh how the path perplexes,
reducing run to plod!
But still self-discipline
forbids my giving in.

Again, as I keep trying
to see what others see,
I wonder if they're lying,
afraid to disagree
with some promoter who,
though shrewd, was baffled too.

Perhaps I'm wrong, but 'here
I stand'. Poetic writing
should have a style that's clear:
obscurity's uninviting.
What's publishing about
if readers feel shut out?

PRODUCTION LINES

An after-life? We hope, but I'm afraid
it's only our dearest myth.
Though generations prayed,
Bach and Milton, along with Brauer and Smith,
were ultimately trash:
we all end up as skeletons or ash.
Yet masterpieces—made by cellwork too,
since brain's the body part we're mindful with—
live on, as lovely as they were when new.

ODD WORK

for Andy Croft

Why this compulsion, Andy? Why oh why
the unrelenting urge that you and I
and other weirdos have, to scribble verse
as though a gift was harbouring a curse?

Everywhere music seems to be, like food,
instinctively accepted; and—though crude
in form and detail, clearly from the heart—
kids' drawings affirm the power of graphic art.

When young we also loved our nursery rhymes,
then schoolyard jingles. Later there'd be times,
pubertal mainly, when the injured soul
might reckon Wordsworth's touch could make it whole.

But when at last intelligence was geared
to adult needs, few readers persevered.
Though rock and pop and pics were still okay,
not many cared what sonnets had to say.

Some rhymers, plainly mad, keep on and on
when hope of being listened to has gone,
trying at least to conjure in the dark
the momentary brilliance of a spark.

G FOR GEORGE

to Gordon Hodgeon

Their blunder, you might say,
was apt in a spooky way.
You won't, like Robert Clive,
have helped proud Brits to thrive;
instead you will have soared
to Parnassus like George Gordon
B, a 'mad bad' lord.

Note: Sadly, Gordon is no longer with us. 'G for George' refers to his poem 'George', included in his collection *Talking to the Dead,* 2015.

BETWEEN POEMS

Not long after the writing, doubt and fear
heap thunderclouds in a sky that had been clear.
Am 'I' two selves, one of whom dares a song
while the other waits, or one now right now wrong
and never knowing which? Is it the shine
of sun or lightning that is truly mine?
Unanswerable questions. All I can say—
though creative will, in searching for a word,
must fly strenuously like a gale-tossed bird!—
is that I love the blue, abhor the grey.

AGAINST FLIGHTS OF POESY

(while reading a poem in twelve cantos)

'Wring the neck of rhetoric' said Verlaine
(rhetorically). Our teacher growled 'Let verse,
however lyrical, be plain and terse.
Use, where you can, five words instead of ten:
prolixity's a curse.'
I've welcomed back those rules while reading more
of Shelley: a rare genius, I don't deny,
but what a pious labour, what a bore
being boosted into a vast platonic sky
by powerful jets of eloquence. Add to that
his lumbering us—though he died at twenty-nine,
for some both all-too-human and divine—
with a book so densely printed and so fat.
Such overdrive! That's blasphemy I admit,
and may the gods forgive me. But whether simple,
subtle, playful or profound,
let poems be guided by Verlaine's example:
metre and rhyme where suitable, but words,
instead of trying to be angels or even birds—
though yes, with unclouded meaning, delightful sound—
staying firmly on the ground.
(You see it's helpful to use the Frenchman's trick
of attacking rhetoric with rhetoric.)

FACING THE EPICS

The student in my dream, a bloke
who, to my id's eyes,
was like the Wimbledon 'wasp' John McEnroe,
said 'How about the heavenly crap
of Homer, Dante, Milton? Can those guys
be serious?' When I woke
there was nothing more, not even the tiniest scrap
of an answer foolish or wise,
so now I'm keen to have a go
at offering one.—First
we might consider the overlap
of musical and poetic symphonies.
I think of someone who, immersed
in verbal sounds, prosodic harmonies,
quite ignorant of Greek, Italian, English,
may find such tones can please
the ear no less than melodies and chords.
But that's a bit like sniffing at a dish
and letting chewy solids go to waste,
for what are joined-up words
without their meanings? These,
if only in translation, give
what cooking's meant to give—the taste
and then the nourishment: that narrative
so rich in images from all the senses,
of heaven and hell, of heroes, spirits, gods,
of passionate impulse and its consequences,
alliances, jealousies, the tempter's trap,
arrogance, vengefulness, the ruck and din
of war on earth, on high, the destined odds
of victory. While treasuring these, we learn
to think about the sap,
moral and theological, within
the branches and the twigs of bygone lore.

But this requires devotion, dogged will.
Agreed, it's wrong to spurn
as fantasy what once was gospel; still,
trudging those miles of myth can be a bore.
Edifying sentiments, prosodic skill,
imaginative genius—it's all there,
and lines like these (don't say it) can't compare.
That's why we sit for hours
honouring cantos, and are grateful for
the editorial notes. But in the end
we feel released. A literary chore,
an effort on the plane of higher powers,
is over. Duty done, we can descend
to humbler levels. *Some* of us. But 'some'
includes, I'm pleased to note, great Doctor J—
how many are gifted with a brain like his?—
who, of the English work, had this to say:
'None ever wished it longer than it is.'
Plain truth where most are circumspectly dumb.
It's one thing coming back to parts we cherish,
another travelling through from start to finish.

    The Italian? The Greek? Old Homer shines
brightest of all! That Dante Alighieri
devoted such creative power to lines
as cruelly punitive as they are scary
still bothers me. We know his mind was fed
on medieval dogma; all the same,
it's sad his genius didn't light a flame
unlike the sort that later
ended Giordano's brave career. To dwell
in canto after canto on the dead
packed in a calibrated cone of Hell—
eternally tortured for their so-called sins,
their all-too-human failings (spare a thought
on *Homo*'s all-too-brutal origins)—
looks virtuously vicious. Who am I
to 'virtuously' criticize and sigh,

given that men were taught
so differently in earlier centuries?
Right; but I'm me, and though I must admire
the *Comedy* I can't love it. Family trees
(cultural here) were hard to do without,
but worried minds from time to time went higher,
flew from the topmost branches, filled with doubt
that what tradition gave was true and kind,
then worded visions challenging the norm.
No intellect, it seems, will ever find
what life is all about,
no bard invent a form
cut off from any that preceded it;
but now and then a poem may appear
that makes a headache for lit crit
and priestly studies too. Will I be here
to greet an epic of our age?
If so I'll give a silent cheer
and hope to love some lines on every page.
    I see now why I dreamed a McEnroe
demanding 'Are they serious?' Can the id
and superego mate? 'The answer's no'
you say. All right, but *something* made a bid
for verses that are free
from heavenly-hellish lore. It spoke for me.

FAME: A DUOLOGUE

Down with poetry—all, that is,
apart from mine. I've had
my bellyful of hers and his,
most of their work so bad
I feel like puking. Yet I've tried
so hard to be 'on poetry's side'.

How is it that such wretched stuff
is globally admired,
line after line so full of guff
yet said to be inspired—
where prosody as well as sense
bears witness to incompetence?

       Shut up, you idiot. We know
       the reason for your gripe
       is that your own stuff doesn't flow
       through any major pipe,
       that nothing from the well of Kell
       can help the world go round like Shell.

Right, I'm a little envious,
but—changing metaphors—
creatures with homes beneath the grass
outlived the dinosaurs,
and some who later swung in trees
eventually sailed the seas.

       Come off it! That comparison
       is utterly absurd.
       In the chronicles of Helicon
       you'll figure as a nerd,
       a humanlike automaton
       who, though his lines were seldom heard
       and hearers' hearts remained unstirred,
       went scribbling on and on.

IV

COLOUR CODING

What a far-left colleague called me,
trying his strength, appalled me,
but 'Wishywashy Lib-Lab Kell'
undoubtedly rang the bell.
In other ways too I think
I'm irredeemably pink.
Not sexually, no:
I'm thoroughly hetero.
But I like the taste of *rosé*
far more than that of, say,
whisky or vodka, and waver
when meat has garlic's flavour.
I find it hard to take
poems that are opaque,
and the sound of atonal works,
to put it mildly, irks.
But enough of that: you get
the point that I'm a wet.

A few blood-reds I knew
were firmly of the view
that laughter's cruel. Yes,
some mirth no saint will bless,
but also there's a kind
not even God will mind,
because he knows the world
he started has unfurled
bright comedy as well
as dark. It can dispel
the gloom, and may be seen
in red, pink, blue, or green—
or all, on a motley bird
who dances the Absurd.

Of that there's lots, our own
as well as others'. Groan
and grin are close as twins,
like gaffes and minor sins.
('To sin'? I much prefer
the unpriestly verb 'to err'.)
Whatever shade we are,
from turmeric to tar,
self-mockery is a boon
that keeps the heart in tune.

Although they were quite clever,
my reddest friends would never
commit, from what I saw,
a chuckle or guffaw,
self-targeted or not.
I suppose the bluest lot—
of whom none ever came
my way—are much the same:
being amused, it seems,
is suspect at extremes.
So I'll stay true to pink,
not on a scowling brink
surmounted by a gun,
but in a dell where fun
can thrive, though sadness too
may wear that gentle hue.

A BIT DEAF

Yes, I have hearing aids—and, being old
in a generous welfare state, I got them free.
But though they're worth far more than their weight in gold
and almost as clever as a dancing bee,
I hardly ever use them. Why? Because,
their fiddliness apart, the conversation
I like is other people's, a friendly buzz
that leaves me free for senile rumination.

TO A WALKING-STICK

My loved ones help me. In my feeble way
I try to help them too.
But they're not always with me, whereas you
are here throughout the day,
patiently waiting for my hand
to grip your strength, as though
you feel and understand.
That's fanciful I know,
but still I count you as a friend
who'll help me with my trudging to the end.

A PLEA FOR ASSISTED DYING (2015)

In ancient China, I've read,
staying alive as long as you can
was greatly valued—at least
so long as you were a man:
about women nothing is said.
Nor is it mentioned that, as years increased,
so did the likelihood
of misery caused by being diseased
or simply exhausted. I wonder why.
You'd think old guys would find it good—
pooh-poohing venerability—instead
of tottering on, to die.
That's how *I*'d feel: being feeble
and therefore no longer able
to do what's useful or pleasant or both,
I'd like to be helped to end
my days, not have to spend
long hours in the wretchedness
of decrepit slump or stress.

Our culture, alas, is loath
to be merciful in that way.
In places abroad you can find a glimmer
of moral and intellectual growth:
some clinics grant you oblivion—if you can pay.
Here, I'm afraid, the story's grimmer:
though few are religious, piety still holds sway.
We love our dogs and our cats,
and when they're in terminal pain
they're kindly 'put to sleep'.
But men and women? That's
entirely different. Each must bear
whatever comes, having as well as a brain

an immortal soul whose journey's in the care
of God. Perennial awe
runs like underground water, deep
in the strata of the law:
for us 'being put to sleep' is like being slain.
Such nonsense! Dear legislators, have a heart!
Help those for whom life is deathly to depart.

CHARITIES

This weariness is more than the sleepy kind.
Not far from ninety, troubled but resigned,
I've been hobbling to the shops
at a tedious mile an hour or so, with stops
for rest. Back in my house, I find the mail
includes another appeal
for money to help the frail,
the hungry or thirsty, the maimed.
Like previous ones, it makes me feel ashamed
of being so safe and cosy. Now I open
a second envelope.
What's this? Dear God, I'm eyeing
a page that begs support for Assisted Dying.

THINKING OF DEATH

Thank you for asking how I am.
Truth is, now being eighty-eight,
therefore well past my use-by date,
I'll soon require my second pram.
By definition still alive,
like younger folk I have to strive;
but calls for action irritate,
light duties having put on weight.
Feeling the grind's not worth a damn,
I won't protest if God or Fate
says 'fuck off'—or, less crudely, 'scram'—
then gives the nod for 'terminate'.

Apologies: I'm filled with shame
for writing those ungrateful lines—
so cynical, so flippant too,
and only from one angle true.
See how another facet shines!
The theme it shows is Me-and-You,
whose Us can take in more than two
at any time when family, friends
and local helpers come to mind.
No man's an island: one life ends
but several feel the shock; and so
an oldster, even if resigned
to final sleep, should try to be
far-sighted when it's time to go:
all humans share the pronoun 'me'.
And while he still can walk, I hope
that though he finds it hard to cope,
his flesh decaying, his spirit dim,
he'll do his damnedest to be kind
to all who have been kind to him.

LIBERATION

If you are near the end,
apprehensive, ailing,
chuck the old paradigm!
Think of life failing
(cellwork undone by time),
of death as a dear friend.

LETTING GO

It's good, said the monolith,
to know my Self will die,
though only through slow wearing
in wind and rain. Why
cling to the foolish myth
of heaven—that you'll go on
from death, proud You for ever?
I find that notion scaring!
Were you an automaton
you'd feel no pain, would know
nothing. But think of a river
made conscious that its flow
would never reach an ocean
to merge with ... Perhaps you'll say
eternity's not duration:
it's timelessness, and the way
to that is mystical,
beyond all cerebration
and sense of self as well.
Yes. Though grand, be humble.
As the long hours go by,
this monumental I,
thank God, will slowly crumble
under the whispering sky.
And after? Who can tell?

A FRIENDLY FIASCO

In hospital for the last time
I was too weak to write
on the registration form.
My dear son kindly obliged.
At *Religion*, to my prompting,
he entered 'None', then added
'Agnostic' in round brackets.
It therefore surprised me when,
on the critical day, a priest
appeared beside my bed.
Polite as ever, I gasped
'I'm sure you're good and kind,
but also I think—forgive me—
that you're deluded.' He smiled,
recited a bit of Latin
and made above my head
the sign of the cross. Amused,
I was careful not to say
'Thanks for the mumbo-jumbo.'
I muttered 'Who knows, who knows?'
Then each of us went his way.

AN ANXIOUS REPLY

The trials of old age I sing,
being almost, now, sans everything.

Parts active or at rest complain—
arms, legs and shoulders all in pain.

Not far from crippledom, I creep.
The stairs are torturingly steep.

My hearing's dull. Half blind, I peer
at shapes no longer bright and clear.

Eating, I have no appetite:
there's drudgery in every bite.

Even companionable talk
can be a task at which I balk.

In short, I find that being awake
is a multiplex diurnal ache.

So what I like to do is snooze,
free for a while from old-age blues.

Believe me, friends, I'm deeply grateful
and hope this answer won't seem hateful:

Though 'Yes, do come' is what I say,
please show your love by staying away.

A NOTE ON THE TITLE OF THIS BOOK

'The whispering sky' is a phrase taken from my poem 'Letting Go' on page 70. The sky has whispered literally with the faint hiss of cosmic background radiation (detectable by instruments), and metaphorically as a prolific inspirer of mythical, quasi-scientific, and sometimes truly scientific ideas.